# SHE SPEAKS | POETRY

edyka chilomé

Para Xochitl y Mayra

And for *She* who has been too scared
to tell of her inheritance and her becoming

# Table of Contents

# Introduction

When I fist learned to speak who I was, it came out in
the language of poetry. Since then, I have found the
courage to tell my stories out loud on stages in my
communities and eventually all around the country.
Years later, I've learned that I have the right to speak,
take up space, and exist just as I am in all of my painful
and beautiful truth. I wrote this book to tell you that you
do too. I give you my written truth in stories, some
written in big words, others in rhymes, many in
contradictions. I lay down all of my complexity in these
pages as an invitation. May you read my rage, my
prayers, my hopes, my passion, my spirit and consider
the urgent need to produce reflections of your own
realities, no matter how painful or surprising
they may be.


Inlakech.

# BOOK ONE |

I'm learning to translate the best of me
In order to tap into the rest of me

      This is not for your entertainment

I'm training the beast in me
constructed by my own imaginary

      This is not for your entertainment

These words are rhythmic reminders
of my existence, my persistence
My fight for breath to be free

Life calling out for itself
        The way I have learned to bleed

This is not for your entertainment

This is for your livelihood

Remedies for your swallowing silence
for moments you never thought you could
never imagined you would

I'm calling you out

Locked doors
Wide open
Bleed with me

This is not for your entertainment

Don't let your insecurities feed
the silence they breed inside of we
Come live outside that prism and believe
we speak words outside of time
We have sight outside of mind

Do you hear me yet?        Do you see me yet?

We are not meant for their entertainment

Our words bleed realities
they must come to reconcile

We are collecting the fragmented pieces
they would otherwise come to file:

        a d d i c t i o n

And I'm scared, just like you

that I have no room to move
in this reality

no end

that I have not been groomed
for their

stages
pages
puzzles
and pens

The only difference is I learned
to make amends when

Audre said:

"poetry is not a luxury"

and breaths are not guaranteed

so while you're on this ride with me

why can't we do more than

look cute and smile?

| ~~I am my mother's child~~

| I Walked Here On My Mother's Back

Each cardboard
and plastic bottom
waits for me
to try again

invites me
to contain myself

holds me in transitions
follows me for miles
cross unfamiliar earth

follow seasons
weather storms
pack light
watch rows
of troubled corn

stare out of
moving windows
unforgiving

studying the
colors of my
ancestors

whispering prayers
with uncertain
intentions


| Haciendo Camino

I have grown invisible
in my wordlessness
hungry in my stillness
idle in my loneliness

~~I have been scared~~
I am scared

of being judged
of seeming foolish

mostly of who I
might come to find
beyond the silence

| Confessions

White sheets. Long shirts, glasses, cloth napkins
Motel room smells. Smoke. Airports. Wild hair
Fruit by the side of the road. Empty homes, dirty
windows, and fresh paint. Ocean pools. Trucks
Open air. Back Alleys. Rain. Silence. Car rides
Silence. Strangers. Letters. Pews. Empty churches
Haunted hallways. Dusty basements. Tears
Sadness. Sadness. Bike rides and sleepovers
Matching clothes and hangovers. Dreams. Late
mornings. Late nights. Songs. Dreams, pianos and
tablecloths. Small pastries and lemonade. Tall trees
and shade. Books. God. Libraries. School
auditoriums . A recorder. A radio. Jessica

| Untitled

I was born into
        revolution

too much hurt
to heal at once

She does not call
   text
       email

     She labors in war

         She moves

away from me

     unable to give birth

        to mother

   | Country of Origin

Rattle
loud
so loud
wailing, screaming
so loud
reckless, unsettling
aggressive
but not present
Not here. Not real
the sounds are not real
big white man laughing
got me all figured out
smiles as deep as bowls of candy
sitting on desk
few feet
many worlds
empty, unsafe
tears and big words
too big for these white walls
their Jesus
their cross


| Zion, Age 12

Tears
 write
  words
     on
      round
         sticky
            canvases

            held
            up
              by
                staggering
                   breaths

                    and
                       lucid
                      memories of
                           suicide

         | She Speaks For Herself

For certain
I know God is love

For certain I know
I manifest
the truth of God
In my being

For certain I know
my fragmentations
are love letters
written to my soul
so it may learn to wake
in the most fragile
and beautiful
parts of itself

For certain
I know my mind
is scared
to meet God
where words
are not enough


| What Is Known

To be clear

I am not your token
to ride a feel good
diversity train

I am me

If you are fearful
of my complexity
or are confused
by my agency

I suggest
you take it up
with your elders
and their many
decisions
that have
blurred
the ways
you see

Also

I don't need
your saving

I am free

| Dear White Savior Industrial Complex

Unthreatening safe  love
open wide  love
friendly Kool-Aid smile  love
patience in your spirit and
kindness in your words  love
nonjudgmental innocent  love
first day in Mr. Turner's class  love
where God is present and
all things matter  love
I don't have to pretend to be different
because I'm enough  love
apart of the post up crew
because we all ghetto but kind  love
I see you and you see me  love
make believe school  love
we are growing  love
we are learning  love
Mama J is our teacher  love
once upon a season  love
we hold out our hearts and
our invitations  love
come to my quince  love
I will never forget you  love

| Sweet Impressions

She slowly wakes

    from the dreams

  born in the belly

        of her father

   She is broken

      misaligned
   torsida
twist
   turn
      every

  position

unnatural

pain   constant

  desperate

she pleads

   "How far is home?"

| Seeking Alignment

# BOOK TWO |

You member
summer daze
we would
run around
the hood **13**

       slowing down

wasn't  a concept

we were able to conceive

    ~~You got locked up~~

      | They captured you

We watch fear
translate on our streets
young mindless armies
Starbucks cups
little dogs in sweaters
eyes that don't see

They love the idea of
living down the street
from a pupuseria
its so cool
ethnic
cute
cheap

Fried chicken and
Chinese food
at a carryout?

Just like T.V!


| Erasure, Repeat Offender

We have learned to define in silence

not out of fear, out of understanding

| On the use of "They" and "Them"

If light equals good and dark equals bad
then if I want to be light is that good or bad?

They told me I was cute for dark
but cousin was beautiful for light
They told me to stay out of light
to be less dark like cousin

They told me light was good so stay in dark
I like the light so I watch from dark
tempted to be beautiful like light cousin

I often wonder where my dark came from
Its hard to find stories of dark
since the world became enlightened

They tell me dark doesn't exist
it is only defined by the absence of light
So maybe my dark is from a time
where there was not light
Maybe in that space
they were not scared of dark

Maybe that's where all my existence be
Maybe there I didn't have to hide from light
to be beautiful like light cousin
Maybe there I could be just me
both and neither, light and dark
maybe there light is good
and dark is free

| A Bright Evening

8 dollars
empty belly
white washed
reality

Revolution
in high
definition

Manufactured
intentions
dressed up in
familiar words

like
hunger

like
games


| For Our Entertainment

Mimic
Laugh
Deny
Laugh
Mimic
Deny
Deny
Laugh
Mimic


| Alg. [{Survive}]

Thousands of years

of becoming
        into nothing

We thirst for something

The sound of a      distant language

      name
      continent
      hero


echoes

      of emptiness

          remedies for our

      bitterness

      melody

   rhythm
touch
look

   kiss


| 2nd Period, Study Hall

We was cool
pre tattoos
pre Mary
pre failin school
pre gangs
pre prison
pre deaths
before you
overdosed
on the cool
we smiled
laughed like child
and dreamed of
a tomorrow
we could
never guess


| Hoodology

She watched
as the   child
she   birthed

    slowly  died

  and  slowly

  killed

her


| Strategies of War

# BOOK THREE |

Dreams of white picket fences

Whispered prayers on deaf ears

You have come so far from God

So close to the United States


| Lost Generation

We exist          invisible

residue bastard children of
          rape and murder
dreadful reflections
          of history                              they do not claim
                                        but act upon gloriously
Tired eyes plead
for humanity          for belonging

Painfully
          displaced
lost
    we are forgotten
old property          enemies

toys that have grown old
and boring          shamed and ridiculed

Our existence
          is questioned
Curious they stare at us

          unfamiliar memories

"Where did you come from?
Why are you here?"


| Phil 321: Articulation, Mobility, and Survival

I sit in a padded wooden chair
on the third floor of a library

I sit across an androgynous dark skinned beauty
with enough music in their bones to make
every closed book in the library dance

They struggle to hear their heart
trapped in a place void of music

They are not convinced of this place
not convinced of the silence that
has seduced our elders

Why should they be?

There is a revolution outside

I sit in a seat next to a man whose curl patterns
speak of continents colliding with so much chaos
and beauty he is crowned Black Indian:
the meeting of warriors, survivor of the
slave ships and the badlands

He sits honoring the coming of a new season

My kin, deep spirit, luminous smile

I open a new window
Staring into blurred reflections
desperately chasing the fading sky

I sit longing for teacher

Yet I have learned well to oblige
to hold still, to survive

There is a revolution outside

Bearing crushing weight
five thousand years
everything to fear

Like water
　　　we hold still

teetering in raging silence
knowing against our will
we have  been conjuring
the revolution inside

it has been dancing

in our memories

on our keyboards

in our eyes

| Field Notes

I remember

your selling of

flesh

your building of

empire

I remember

our dying

cracked earth

grey water

black sky


| Amerika

I'm from immigrant dreams
Born amidst war and faded stories

of rape and guerrilla warfare

I come from instinctual survival

Creativity caught in 22 or
15 children with no shoes
who witness Mami getting beat
in the other room

only to hear over and over again:

"This is where we come from
this is who you'll be"

Villages killed and teachers hung

by U.S. trained military

We've been trained

to hold our tongues

to become field slaves
who hunger in the night
for a new visionary

thinking freedom
is still to come

We believe freedom is still to come

So we sleep and bathe
in the stench of this
American dream

knowing that in reality

I come from need
to survive so that
we may live

so that I may give
and belong
if not to a family
than to a struggle
and a song

if not to my mother
then to mi pueblo
and these poems

See I was raised
on the memories
of my people
so that I may
know them

so that I may
remember

I come from
border crossing

crushing silence and the
desperation of belonging

from broken hearts and minds
but fighting spirits

Always fighting

En la lucha    no hay de otra

Si se puede!   Si se puede seguir

in this never
ending desire
to be something more
than lost childhood dreams
more than child of child
who knew no tenderness
in their seams

who cannot name
their tears

who are without
the privilege
of living

without

fear

You see

I come from
the need to survive

so that we may live

Pero me dicen:

*"Oye niña quien tiene*
*tiempo para justicia*
*si tengo que limpiar esta casa*
*y darle de comer a mi familia*
*antes de ir a mi segundo trabajo!"*

They tell me:

*"Yo Erica! Who has time*
*for justice anyway*
*when all we have is*
*just us and a payday!"*

I say, true

But to answer your question

I have not found my home
in a city or a place

Rather I have seen
my seeds sown
and grown
in the potential
of this here page

So in the midst of it all
all you really need to know is
I was raised on hope

that the living
would come alive

That we could do more
then just survive
so that I could stand here
and look in your eyes
to remind you
in case you may
have forgotten

tu eres mi otro yo

You are my other me

So you better find
your place in this struggle
because it's about that time
for our people

to live

free

| #Y    eCanse

They gave us permission
to go back to the land
from which you came

Sold us a ticket to see
the ruble of what remained

We traveled across the growing deserts
and the velvet green
Ancestors long forgotten
and never seen

We arrived with nothing in hand
amidst the vestiges of war

We inhaled overgrown cities
uncertain of what we were looking for

We watched them traffic the land
and crawl the sky

We sat with elders tasked
to watch the earth die

We remembered your songs
under the bright shifting sky

We remembered your aging faces
your oceans opened wide

| Stories Of Diaspora

If I am short in my messages
it is because I am unsure how
to communicate my sentiments respectfully

It might be that I have una mecha corta
yet I can't help but feel like at times
we are both too impatient for our own good

I remember my words the last time I saw you
I remember just how deep I meant them to cut
how explosive our tears were
as they met our hands

A language separates us
but we are molded the same

I translate your passion for expression
into boom baps that swing
like jazz in the summer
and you look at me in unfamiliar ways

You ask me why I talk such a foreign tongue
why I write my story in the books of others
as if there is no room for you on those pages

I am your story viejo

I write your book in a language you cannot read
but if you'd look at me you'd see
I am clothed in the same joy and shame
you have already seen and lived

Yet I am living

I am your mirror in a foreign land
you have tried to make home

Yet still too, I am the home that
 first welcomed you

dirt floors and straw roof

I am the shoes that you wore so proudly on your
feet when you had no other promise of dignity

I am the feet that took you to sea
that stepped on a land far away
from what you had always seen

I am the painted concrete that greeted you

The fear that moved you

The courage that kept you
so far for so long from
the land of your mothers

I am your mother too

searching for ways to survive
in a time of violence and hate

Misunderstood
and unnoticed
by those closest to me

I am afraid

I fear my love for her
might make me feel unwoman
unhuman in your house
In my solitude
I give life over and
over again

Yet still, I am the child birthed
of too many wars to count
and too many deaths to remember

I am that which you fear
and which you love so fiercely
inside and outside of yourself

I am you Viejo

Look at me

Take time to listen

carefully

witness

Yo soy el cambio
de cual canto la cantante

haciendo camino al andar

siempre hasta la victoria del amor

de tu corazón al mio

Yo soy tu sangre mi viejo

nunca lo olvidare

y nunca estaré lejos de ti


Tu Hija, La Jota


| Querido Papa

# BOOK FOUR |

She wakes

and our gaze
wraps around whole
continents and ancients seas
to meet peace in the depths
of our satisfied bellies

I feel the safest I will ever be

the musk of sex, sage, and sweet
oils fills me with satisfaction

knowing
we have continued to
birth life

both woman
and non white
daughters of genocide

born in Babylon
we have continued
to survive

| Queer

I cannot be named
nor can I be bound
by   either   or

My flesh is how

I partake in conversation

It is how I theorize
how I remember

how I survive


| Third Space

Angry brown
queer queen
that's what they
been callin me

Even gave me a seat
in the house of royalty
to kill me silently and slowly

Hot headed jealousy
traveled cross seas
only to want to be
what I be, and always been

Don't mess with they paper
but I'm known
to play with a pen

Use their words
to reflect to them
an ugliness that
seeps like poison
and they can't look at me

Avert their eyes
when they see me
with her

We too grown
to claim the ether
but we got it yo!

Always had it
and I know
they've known

So they take back
what they said before

Hold themselves holy
like they headed for

heavens dressed up
in holy ghosts

emulating
shadows of what
we were before?

Yet they can't reach Her

Rape Her on Her back
pretend to save Her
can't let Her go

Still searching for
a pot of gold

So short sighted
so they killin yo

Bombs keep falling
we call each day a miracle

Babies crying, each day
we grow cynical

In the midst of violence
we find life is cyclical

Been reborn
a hundred times
in breech

found humanity
is fickle so

I stay grounded
in the spiritual

Reflections eternal
the cadence is endless
bump the rhyme scheme
they could never end this
So they can never end me

They call me angry
brown queer queen

You can call me E


| Remnants of the Boom Bap

I met her long before papa me dijo
que son unos mal creados
que no quieren trabajar

My affections caught between her
kinky curls and growing baby locks

Before my mother came to work
the fields of this country

Before she gave birth to me
in a ghetto of the northeast
surrounded by hustlers selling
shea butter, body oils, and incense

Her round brown eyes were home
before we moved south in search of
paisas and lower interest

Before I understood how much it cost
to buy the American dream

This was before I bumped chopped and screwed
and spit verses over dollar store notebooks
and into computer screens

Before wet nights came
I dreamt about her

Before my mother asked me
why I talk like a negra

Before my father heard my poems
and said he would always trust
los gringos more

This was before he broke my heart

Before I learned there was no choosing
to be daughters of the enslaved
and assimilated

We are relegated to the same prisons
redlined to the same ghettos
displaced and raped in the same
damned communities

There was no choosing

Searching for God I recognize the stories
of her dark tones, round hips, and wide nose
and when her notes flow, I remember

I give offerings to her ancestors
between warmed sheets and curled toes

I thank them for being witness
to our love, to our desperate
desires to be whole

I thank them for keeping our steps
and giving us music and poetry
to feed our wounded souls

I kiss the corner of her smile

After thanksgiving I sit naked
next an open window
sending prayers to mis antepasados
sage smoke and humble words

I ask for vision while we walk borderlands
as extensions of this colonized
and unfamiliar earth

My heart explains to the moon

There was no choosing
these wet and dark bodies
this creative act of survival

this life giving love

There was only choosing
the path the ancestors gave
between star shine and clay
with no one to celebrate

the love between two sisters


| La India y La Negra

I spoke to an elder the other day
and at some point in the conversation
she pointed up to the moon
and confidently turn to me to say:

*"She has watched over many lovers*
*Traced the paths on which fingers discovered*
*Stimulating, making claims over bodies*
*so as to keep them living. Life giving*

*See in her light skin speaks and lips feel*
*making no sound, in humble and laborious ways*
*Making selflessness a sacrament on every given day"*

She said

*"You see this conversation has long begun*
*but Erica, when you write you should try to shed light on*
*the underground because to them our graves have been*
*done, dressed up in poverty, negation, and denial. But*

(she whispered), *anytime they try to cover up the*
*remains, they leave room for revival*

*And that is why we lay. In her light we tell stories*
*with no sight and no gaze, hidden from the power*
*of his day, we find refuge in her night*

*Always remember we live rebirth by death*
*and we should always, always*
*seek each other to take flight"*

And just like that, I finally understood
why I longed to touch you

And if I could be so bold in this poem
if you only knew what your breath
and your moan do, you'd be so
lost in my liberation you'd forget
all that our people have gone through

Inherit pain and memories
would dissolve into present day glories
manifested in the ways you choose to
explore me and my people's past

When you find the courage to do that
our lives no longer fit in their hour glass

And the struggle of my mother's becomes
so clear in the friction between your fingers
and my skin, mestizaje becomes
the only language our love is born in

The way you caress my back
you'll learn of where my souls been

If you trace my scars
you'll learn of my father's sin

But don't worry, we're free from his lies
and his stories because our story is
enacting right now

And this is more than a deep sex poem
these are visions of our liberation right now

So if they try to say this is not revolution
I would challenge and ask them how

Because in my skin, and in your skin, the proof lies
that our ancestors are still livin

So when we praise that, we are only giving
praise to where praise is due

And as long as the moon still shines

I will allows find a way for my skin to speak

and let you know

that I love you


| Meztli

I held her hands as we stood
We professed our love
in the place of our birth

Ancestors greeted us, sent us flowers
pressed into bones

They had been waiting for our arrival
waiting to hear us remember

waiting to feel our return


| Ocean

From the cradle of the beginning
to the womb of the flood
from the nest of the singing
to the walls of the bud
bloomed beautiful with the promise
of new day, neueva vida
formulated out of new clay
molded into the streams
that once drew life
that once knew rivers
and great strife
oceans abound but
even the great expanse drains
into the great mirrors
made of walking talking veins
to take it home once again
to where perfection transcends
caught somewhere before
the beginning and after the end

| Atl: Ual

# BOOK FIVE |

We have been made

to forget

a wet world

full of wombyn

full of

love

full of


flesh


| Cyborg

Sensible to intuition

blocked by fragmentation

blows to the head

>blood on the earth

We are
>numb to pain

We have only known
tenderness
>at a price

paid

>every 3 minutes

>every 15 seconds

>with our lives


| Neurosis

Do you
See me
Human
Do
You see
Me
Human
I am
Wombyn
Flesh & blood
I am
I am
I am
You
You are
Me


| Broken Mirrors

We lay down
under neon lights
trace bodies of our fathers
offer our wounded limbs
gather our tortured memories

gaze up at the white void

staggering pulse

We no longer sleep
We watch death

over and over again


| Night Shift

Hands full of watercolor teardrops

she whispers:

"More than I want to be pretty

I want to be human"

| Buzz Cut

Standing between
bitterness and death

between fear and
childlike courage

my heart drowns in
naivete and starshine

searching for stories

of the ancients


| Super Power Choice #3

My sisters claim homes in
crumbling buildings
no locks no doors
constant shooting
trapped in open bodies
anxiety becomes daily breath
sleep transforms into contradiction
a necessity a danger
stranded misery
no where to move
outside of war

| I Don't Watch the News

I have been mourning in transition

    mourning the change in the season

      the breaking of the seed

the loss of the night

    the coming of the day


| Coatlicue State

Before she began to tend to her humanness

she called herself an activist

She spent time
banging on walls
forcing doors open

desperatley
searching
 for
self

She played

activist

like a child

plays dress up

                      She doesn't do that anymore

| The Other Side of The Pillow

When she turns to me
with rivers rushing down
the sacred mounds on her face

When she asks me why they
push her down as she stands
as she waits, pull her hair
as she listens and creates
touch her spirit in uncomfortable ways
and attempt to defile her sacred place

If she dares to ask me why she feels so
worthless and empty inside I will say

We exist in a war

one we have not lost yet

And I am sorry my child for the wounds
you have already met

I am shamed that I cannot protect you
from the games they have set

But remember this

Your silence will not save you

Your blood is not to be feared

You are human and you are here

And I will walk beside you
in this war zone

I will remember your tears
and your heavy heart

I will hold you and love you
till the sun meets the dark

And our love
will always be
our greatest weapon


| Mija

Endowed with the power of life
through human form
I am charged with the task
of making sure my sisters and brothers
are warned that there must be room for new life

new forms of existence, new heights
consider the breaking of the seed
and its desire to be ripe in order to
start all over again

In order to start all over again
I take to paper and pen in hopes
that you will hear me

In hopes that
you will see me

In hopes that you
might remember

May we remember
to hear stories of women
who are silenced and not voiceless

May we be courageous

May we be courageous enough
to hear ghetto children's voices
who know survival as a creative act
found in rhythms beaten into desks and walls
in over crowded classrooms on the south side

Or in the ink that covers their wounded bodies
who encounter the price of war and poverty
every day of their lives

May we remember their lives are shaped
by how much their life is valued
or systemically thrown away
and they inherit and manifest
every memory born of women of color today who
have been deemed too poor and savage
to behave as mothers

May we remember the countless women of color
who have had their children removed
from their care by state forces

Because they could not afford divorces
from their abusers, users, 501c3's
and other government entities
who will count their heads
and write their poverty porn stories
for your consumption

May we remember

the queer women of color
struggling to build healthy families
and communities without access
to basic liberties like walking outside
without the threat of being left to die
in the back of a convenience store
in Houston, Texas

May we remember

the women of the global south
who put trembling hand to weeping mouth
when they found their children
had been kidnapped and sold
by American and European
adoption agencies

May we never forget

the long history and
present day reality
of women of color who are
sterilized without their consent
in the clinics, prisons, and colonies
of this so called land of the free

May we work hard

to honor the children of color
who have confused their desire to have child
with their desire to have love
their families could not offered
to give them four generations
over due to

                        mass incarceration

                  economic displacement

gentrification and systemic poverty

May we be courageous enough to recognize
we are both the villains and heroes
in these stories of reproductive tragedies

May we see our reflections in those
who have been deeply wounded
by our violent fantasies of excess
and economic freedoms

May we tell stories that complicate and humanize
instead of simplify and victimize
no matter how much courage it takes

In the words of sister Aja Monet

may we be courageous

may we be courageous

may we be courageous


| There Are No Cards
        This is Not a Game

# BOOK SIX |

Red truck

Hot sun

Windows down

Selena blastin


| San Anto Summer

I remember the day I learned
that my mother and my mother's mother
made 20 cents an hour in their lifetime

It was the same day I realized
the descendants of those who survived
the worst genocide known to human kind
were still expected to be slaves

slaves in a culture that would force them
to live off of 20 cents an hour
that's one dollar a day
only to be called illegal aliens
and maids who clean the houses
of "human" women
who are privileged enough
to ask for equal pay

I remember the first time I attempted
to commit suicide I was eight

trying to find a place to exist
between my mother's tired tears
and blue eyed Amerikan hate

It was before I learned that
my net worth could increase if I
straightened my hair
kept silent and barley ate

10 years later I wonder

if my brown body
was already priced
when capitalists decided
that my wild savage life
was less profitable than land
they would never come to really know

Or if my children's children
will recognize
their grandmother's
indigenous faces
in appropriated patterns
found on white people's clothes

I wonder

if in seven generations
we will still have to sell
the remaining pieces
of our wounded souls
to be guaranteed another day

Or if our descendants
will still be made to believe
that our native traditions
are primitive
but buying back our clothes
from corporations
like forever 21
is some how okay

I wonder

if Euro American people will continue
to be guaranteed the consumption
of our ancient temples, cultures, and lands
without connecting them to displaced
and exploited brown hands in their kitchens

I wonder

if in 7 generation my descendants
will look down at their brown skin and
ancient eyes to remember they are children

of Maya              Aztec
          and Inka
  Cado            Lenca
and   Choctaw            Tioga
              Pueblo
      Huitchol          y Quechua

children of turtle island America

descendent of those who turned the earth
and sowed the seeds. Honored the water
and protected the trees

Born from the breath of healers and dreams

children of spiritual warriors

        that fought for life to be free

I wonder

if they will continue to be forced to work
in a world where their life is defined by numbers
and their bodies imprisoned and sold
by the millions in the name of
liberal progression and freedom

I wonder

if being equal to their "competitors" in this
nihilistic game will only force them
to be just as vain
                    and forget

forget to look at the protectors
of our world
                    the vast horizon

            the sun and the sky

and the beauty that lies

in the wombs

of their grandmother's

memories


+ HISPANIC

Ancestors

Speak

louder


Speak

louder

still


| Sóri-táu Turúbe

Thick waist
dark hair
brown skin

Strong legs
round thighs
long limbs

Hanging breasts
ancient face
waved curls

Soft belly
wet lips

distant worlds


| Obsidian Mirror

They have told us
stories of a house
with no doors
to walk through
no windows
to see through
no roof
no sky
no dirt
no universe
no hope
no color
no love

this is

no

home

of mine


| The Master's House

We stepped to the fire holding out offerings
stretching our tongues like nets

We hoped to catch words that mirrored
the emotions swimming in
the heavy pools of our spirits

I did not hold back the tears
I did not correct the fear in my voice

Nor did I feel ashamed of the desperation
in my fumbling prayer

It has taken so long to find myself here

I stood next to my sisters
I had nothing else to lose
I was not the only one

The women have been gathering

We have come to meet the fire
We have come to ask the questions
We have come in search of

home


| On the Red Road

We have traveled this path before

    again and again

I remember this land

    again and again

The land of my mothers

    again and again


| Atzlan

# BOOK SEVEN |

I have seen the
Holy Spirit work

She lives and
breathes in bodies
dressed in ancient colors
spilling miracles
from their mouths
born of unforgiving secrets

She speaks prophecies
tells of mothers who conjure
grief and anger into
magic and medicine

She labors in pain
waiting to be born from
the mouths of daughters
who are finding
the courage to

speak

| The Revival

Clear the rubble

Plant the seeds

A new season is coming

| After the Riots

We have been watching
We have been watching you paint
colorful and creative visions
for the survival of our worlds

We are watching you mold
and transform the clay of
shattered bodies, places of war
and poisoned rivers

We watch you keep the sacred fire
your hearts open, our spirits warm

We watch your quiet words
your loving actions
your ancient eyes

We are watching your
fingers come alive
like water, ripples of
creation and time

We are watching your passion
y coraje settle into waves
of nourishing wisdom
and we will watch you
change form, transition
back to the creative spirit
the source of your grace
your beauty and your colors

| Dear Mothers

He has been known

by many names

many forms

Yet

his blue prints

remain
written

on the walls

of your womb

| Santificado Sea Su Nombre

Before your daughter
meets the God
that asks
her
to apologize
for
her nakedness

remind her

that she was born

of water

made of stardust

and miracles

sculpted

by the memories
of her ancestors

Tell her

that she is magic
that red blood will seep
from in between her legs
like sap

from the trees

a covenant
        made by her mothers

reminding her that
she belongs
to the cycles
of our earth

and all that is alive
is
her
inheritance

Tell her
that
her pussy
is
sacred

that in time she will learn
her clitoris
brings her
closer to
her creator

Tell her
her breasts
are soft reminders
that indeed she is
a creator
too

Tell her

that every part
of her
is
on purpose

like the ocean and the sky
the moon and the tides
and the infinite colors that

speak
her
name

Before

she learns shame

tell her
that the need to hide is
not
her doing
but the doing of stories
told by those
who are jealous
of

her magic

| Before Your Daughter Learns Shame

We have survived your torching
and your genocide

We have already told you
that we are alive

and my God

you should be happy
that we are humble enough

to respect

our creator

| Que Dios Te Bendiga Hermano

She is constantly learning tongue
Constantly trading energies with her sisters
like it's the end of the month

She is forced to prioritize
the creative act of survival

She walks carefully and intentionally
on a daily with all the courage
she has ever known

She cries
She bleeds
She is constantly trying
to remember that she is everything
that has never been seen

that she is magic
that she is the reflection
of every woman
that has ever spoken

and all the universes
that have ever been
born through war

She is often tired


| Spiritual [Art]ivist

Yo soy la mujer
que nacio del agua
las estrellas
y la luna

La mujer que chupa la herba sagrada
mujer
que recuerda

Yo soy la mujer que llora
la mujer que sana
que habla
y que lucha

| Mujer Espiritu

BOOK EIGHT |

There is a new love born in me
each time I witness the darkness
right before the sunrise

| Faith

He said
                "you float in colors"


I told him      it's all


        I have ever seen


Hues

    of undecided          inspiration

                    Liquid shades        of content

                                Pigments

                        deep enough to hold

heartbreak

        prayers

                and regret


| De Colores

May we continue to serve
as reminders to each other
that we are not alone or forgotten

amidst colorless war, amidst death

May that thought become
the places we desperately seek
to keep our spirits protected

nourished and wet


| Hueltiuh

All of it matters

All of its valid

All of it holds place


| Truth

Remember. We will find home
again. It will exist in the depths
of compassion again
in the euphoria of love
we will build it with courage
again and again. We will rest
in the roots of our intentions
If we dare to survive this war
We must remember to choose
love again and again
Remember

| If I Go Missing

I am eternally grateful to my communities
and ancestors who served as midwives in the
birthing of this book.

Tlazokamati. Shapanayán.

# edyka chilomé

is a national speaker, spoken word artist, writer, MC, and spiritual activist. She holds a B.A. in social and political philosophy with an emphasis in social justice from Loyola University Chicago and an M.A. in Women's Studies from Texas Women's University. Beyond that, she is human and likes to hear from other humans.

edyka.chilome@gmail.com

52651423R00064

Made in the USA
Charleston, SC
23 February 2016